# I Love You More

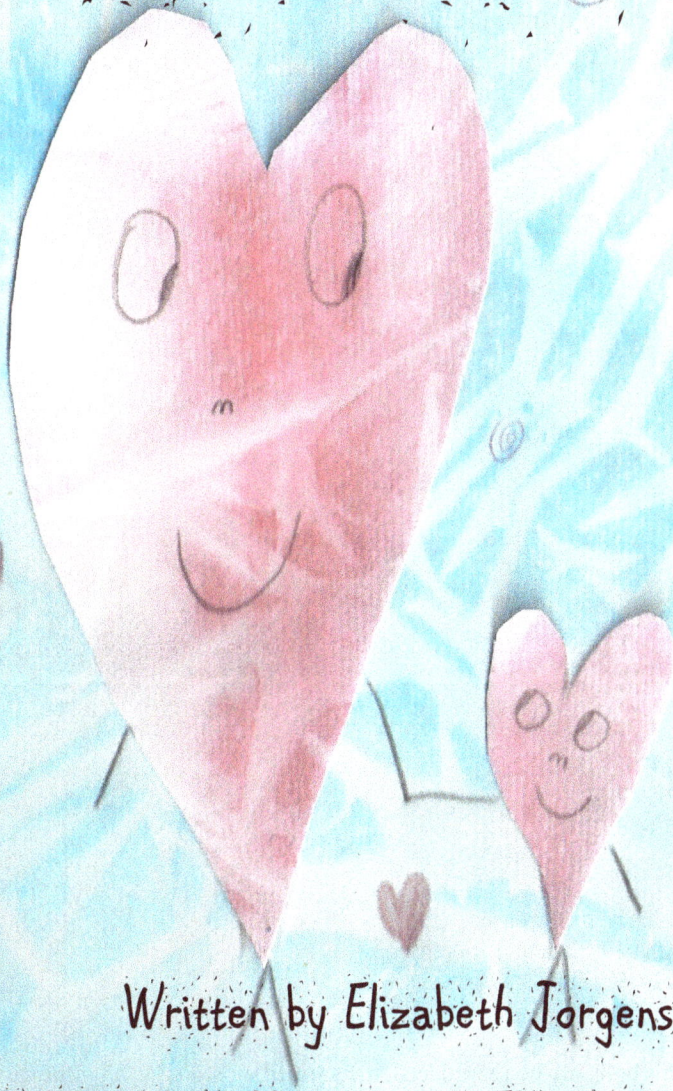

Written by Elizabeth Jorgensen

Illustrated by Hannah and Elizabeth Jorgensen

Publishing History
KDP  Paperback edition 2012
Ingram Spark Hardcover edition 2019


Paperback edition ISBN-13 978-1479233380
Paperback edition ISBN -10  1479233382
Hardcover edition ISBN 978-0-578-58024-1

Dedicated with all my love

to my two beautiful daughters,

my little inspirations

I love you more

Than all the snow on the alps

I love you more

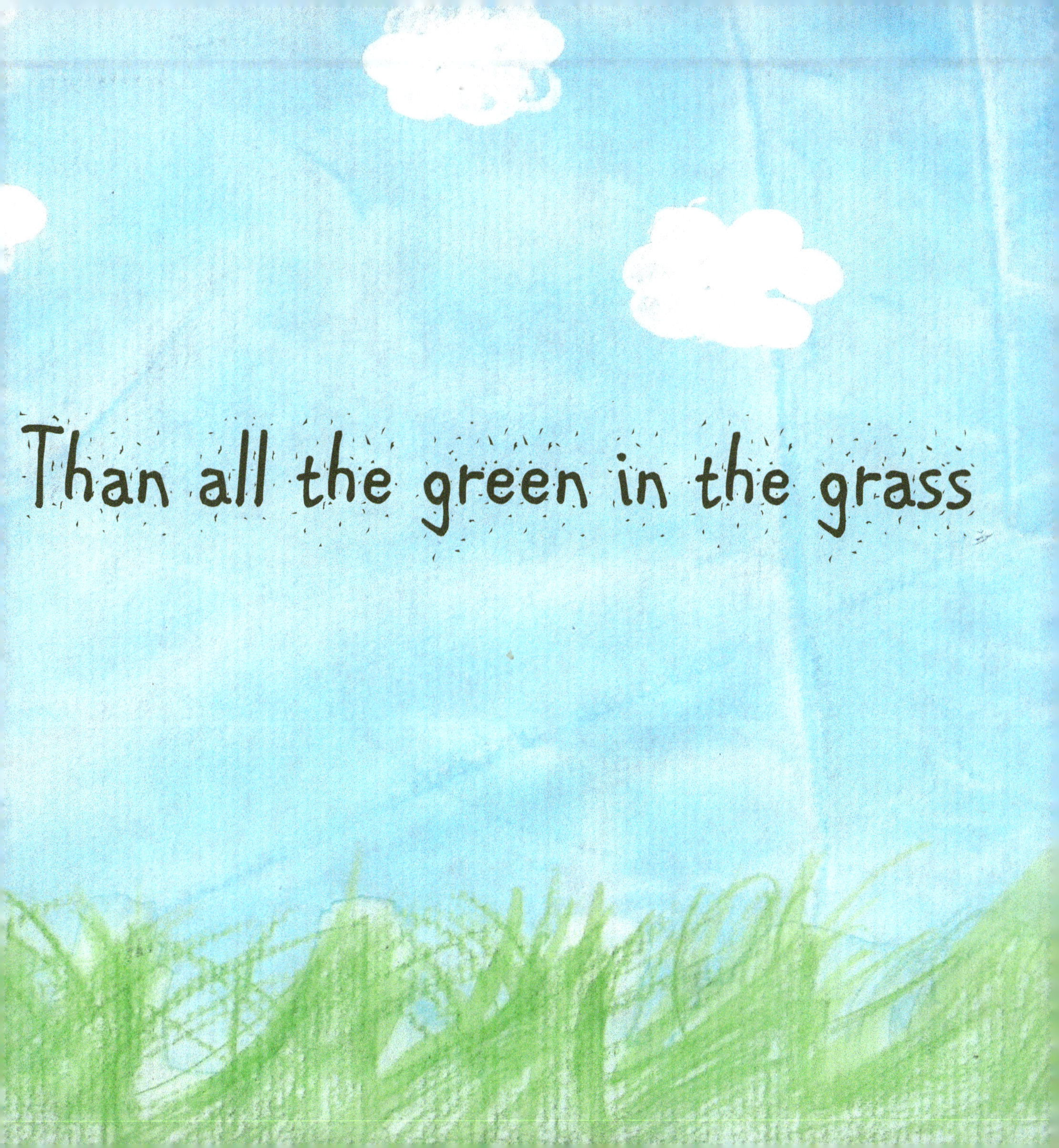

Than all the green in the grass

I love you more

Than all the dark in the night

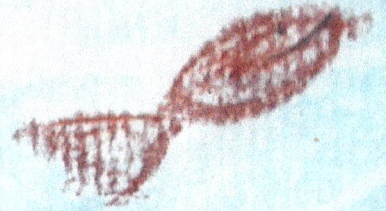

I love you more

Than all the water in the ocean

I love you more

Than all the sand in the desert

I love you more

Than all the colors in the rainbow

I love you more

Than all the stars in the sky

I love you more

Than all the fire in the sun

I love you more

Each and every day!

www.ingramcontent.com/pod-product-compliance
Lightning Source LLC
Chambersburg PA
CBHW062006090426
42811CB00005B/768